Hov Married & Not Kill Your Spouse

Powerful Ways to Deal with Difficult Spouse, Cultivate Happiness in an Unhappy Marriage, & Boost Intimacy

By

Claire Robin

Other Books by the Same Author

I want to thank you for purchasing this book. Below are other books that will also help in boosting intimacy and improving your marriage positively:

1. 200 Ways to Seduce Your Husband: How to Boost Your Marriage Libido and Actually Enjoy Sex: A Couple's Intimacy Guide

2. 232 Questions for Couples: Romantic Relationship Conversation Starters for Connecting, Building Trust, and Emotional Intimacy

3. Communication in Marriage: How to Communicate Effectively With Your Spouse, Build Trust and Rekindle Love

4. Anger Management in Marriage: Ways to Control Your Emotions, Get Healed of Hurts & Respond to Offenses (Overcome Bad Temper)

5. <u>100 Ways to Cultivate Intimacy in Your Marriage</u>: How to Improve Communication, Build Trust and Rekindle Love

6. <u>40 Bible Verses to Pray Over Your Husband and Marriage:</u> Powerful Scriptural Prayers for Protection, Guidance, Wisdom, Companionship, Commitment, Healing, and Deliverance

7. <u>Sexual Intimacy in Marriage:</u> 100 Facts Nobody Ever Told You About Sex and Romance [FREE BOOK]

8. <u>How to Build Trust in a Relationship:</u> Powerful Ways to Rebuild Effective Communication, Resolve Conflict, Improve Intimacy, And Avoid Betrayal

9. <u>How to Deal with Husband's Pornography Addiction:</u> Powerful Ways To Help Your Spouse To Overcome & Recover Completely, While Improving Your Sexual Intimacy

10. How to Deal with A Difficult Spouse: Regain Control, Living with a Demanding, Manipulative, and Unappreciative Partner

11. How to Repair a Broken Marriage: Get Back On Your Feet, Bring Back the Lost Passion, And Cultivate a Better Relationship

Table of Contents

Introduction 6

Signs of Unhappy Marriage 9

Upgrading Your Relationship Ethics 21

Honing Your Communication Skills 27

Developing Confidence in Each Other 33

You Vs Your Spouse 38

Do The Impossible 44

Final Words 49

Introduction

Even though the society has painted the wrong picture about marriage commitment, resilience, and the amount of matrimonial happiness an individual is entitled to, marriage is one of the most beautiful things that can ever happen to a person. It is apparent that you have to put some work into making your marriage work, but having a long-lasting peace and satisfaction in your marriage relationship is absolutely possible. The fear of failure should be overcome by love, likeness, and the passion to be with this person regardless of the defects or flaws. This book is focused specifically on the powerful strategies that have been experimented among couples to help develop marriage relationship to the deepest. These strategies are being shared by people who have successfully spent significant years in marriage and are still going strong into the love Ville.

Marriage is not a science, but it only requires effective actions relevant to the situation faced by couples. All you need is an extra attention to yourself, spouse and the status of your relationship, and you will end up the happy partner. Once these strategies are applied diligently, couples would never contemplate divorce or marriage counselling because everything will be imperfect perfectly, even as they build great deal of patience toward each other. This will mark the beginning of a happy family and you will never regret marrying this person.

Signs of Unhappy Marriage

Reason #1

When you and your partner know that your marriage needs help and you refuse to get help. Also, when the other partner doesn't want to work on the relationship and you seem to be the only one making an effort. Then you are in an unhappy marriage.

Reason #2

Your partner tends to control everything about you now. You feel like everything you are doing is being watched and regularized by your partner. You are afraid of taking a step without informing your spouse. And every time you do what you want, your partner yells at you.

Reason #3

Your plans have shifted to YOU singular instead of YOU plural. Your priorities have shifted to selfish interests and you don't include your spouse in your plans anymore. Your spouse doesn't include you in his or her plans and you don't seem to bother because you know there is no affection that could bring about harmony or teamwork.

Reason #4

You don't go on date nights anymore. Financial challenge is no more an excuse for not going on date nights but the differences you are beginning to discover. If you don't make plans or stopped thinking about date nights, it is likely your marriage is not moving in the right direction.

Reason #5

You don't spend quality time together anymore and one or both of you don't really bother. Quality time could be created when there is a need for deep conversation and the practice of showcasing affection toward one another. It only stops when you have lost passion for each other.

Reason #6

When you prefer friends instead of your partner for advice or actualization. You can make plans and run along with the plan without informing your spouse.

Reason #7

You feel like you need to talk to someone about your feelings, apart from your spouse, even though you know that you shouldn't. Lack of happiness pushes married individuals toward emotional affair, and this makes them vulnerable to the physical affair.

Reason #8

You don't feel the need to calm your spouse. You don't feel their pains even when they cry about the lack of progress of your relationship.

Reason #9

When you are always defensive, blaming and criticizing. When you don't want to take responsibility for your mistakes, call them or even refuse to pick their calls.

Reason #10

You have now stopped fighting even though nothing has changed. This shows the sign of giving up and infidelity might occur at a slight opportunity. Giving up on the affection you once had is very dangerous.

Reason #11

Your fantasy has shifted from a better life with your spouse to a life without your spouse. This is worst when you have someone else in mind, to spend a life with, to find happiness and emotional attachment. This begins with emotional detachment, which may consist of adjustment of priorities. This often causes irrational decisions when it comes to doing things that might affect your spouse's emotions.

Reason #12

You can vividly feel the distance between you increasing, and all you want to do is to include a third party for help or to end the marriage.

Instead of dealing with your own problems, you are now preoccupied with other people's issues. People with too much problems tend to use other people's problems for mental diversion so they wouldn't have to think much about their problems. Putting enough thought about your problem will help you in finding new ways to solve them.

Reason #13

You begin to ignore your instinct. You just do things out of obligations. You have lost sight of what is wrong to you or what is right. You have lost the sight of your passion or the things you would like to do to add meaning to life.

Reason #14

You are together but you are disconnected. You can't have a real conversation or even connect the you used to. Even when you engage in a conversation it always turns out sour, no matter how you control your emotions.

Reason #15

You are out of words for one another. You can sit in the same room but cannot converse efficiently because you don't feel connected. You can't share stories about your day or work because you don't think they are interested.

Reason #16

Last but not the least, when you are not having sex anymore. Yes, this is the commonest indications and warning signs of unhappy marriage. Sex is a natural need, and excluding it form your marriage means that you are not happy with your relationship, and you do not have the passion to be intimate.

Unfortunately, romance tends to be the first to die in a relationship. In all that you do, make sure you give more attention to your sexual intimacy. Do not allow sex to be absent regardless of the guilt and misunderstanding. Do not allow your partner to get used to not having sex with you.

Upgrading Your Relationship Ethics

Go against the world

Your marriage is not a community project. Stop wasting your time detailing the activities of your marriage to the people outside, not even your friends. Love is crazy and marriage is even crazier. You and your spouse are going to agree with unusual things about teach other that the society will frown upon once they know. So, keep your personal business personal. This is the first commandment of happy and better marriage.

Long-term relationship can only be cultivated when you chose not to be influenced by what people outside say. And people will only have specific opinions when they know exactly what is going on with your marriage. Talk regularly with each other about things bothering your person. Make plans together on how to face a particular challenge. Do not stop from there, act upon your plans together. Your partner will make mistakes, there will be faults, too much faults to count, but you have to remain strong for them, because their win is also your win.

Change the subject of argument

If you constantly feel the need to argue, at least change the topic. Arguing about the same thing every day is childish, and I want to believe that marriage only occurs between adults. You have to stop worrying about the same things over and over. If something is actually bothering you, use the previous strategy to make sure you find solutions together. Push towards a solution to bring about the end of a problem or weakness. Forgive quickly and learn to observe the little improvements your partner is making, either in avoiding fights or by making sure you are not hurt anymore.

Commit and keep committing

Commitment is the most important part of marriage, and there is no shortcut to obligations towards the person you are married to. But commitment has to occur in love and peace. It has to occur with passion and respect for each other. Even as you give all to your spouse, you are not allowed to brag about it to their face or to the people outside the home. You can only grow your relationship through commitment, and happiness will transpire in the process. The more you commit the more you will find reasons to stop committing. But you have to keep reminding yourself that your commitment is the best definition of unconditional love, and you have to keep practicing it before your marriage will work.

Honing Your Communication Skills

You don't always need permission

You don't need your spouse's permission before you do something good. Your spouse should not control what you do or what you don't. Marriage commitment and obligations only demands that your partner should be concerned and caring about the steps you take. There should be a certain level of trust for your decision-making capability. Let there be respect, compromise, patience and good communication, in order to prevent unnecessary disagreements.

Think before you speak

Just because this person is married to you doesn't mean they can't get upset when you run your mouth. You can lose this person. Even if you think they can't leave you, losing their passion, respect and love is as devastating as losing them physically. So it is very important to watch what you say around your spouse and what you say to them. Think things through before you say them. Learn better communication skills so that you can communicate your problems without being accusing or confronting. It is very important that your partner thinks you can be supportive when they admit of wrongs or weaknesses.

Allow for validation

The best place your partner will look for validation is from you. Respect and acceptance is very important in your relationship. Even though you have to disagree with them on certain things, you need to constantly let them know that you mean good by interjecting or going against some of their endeavors. Let your character and action reflects passionate feelings and thoughts. Do not belittle your partner's effort for any reason. Make time for validation, where you will discuss personal issues for the purpose of improving your level of openness, therefore improving your confidence in each other.

Be resilient

There is always the rough side of marriage, and you will need to be strong to overcome each and every obstacle. Sometimes you will be tempted to take a risky step that might destroy your relationship. Firstly, you have to be willing to endure trials and temptations before you can be able to endure. You have to be determined to stay strong, then you will realize the strength in your capability for dealing with problems. You will begin to make better decisions even when your spouse is not around to support or approve of the steps you take.

Developing Confidence in Each Other

The need for each other

Your partner will only slack on their responsibility when they think they don't need to be responsible. They won't have a significant affection toward you when they don't think you notice or need their attention. Everyone just needs motivation. Everyone needs to feel that he or she is being needed to carry out some tasks and that they will be appreciated after they accomplish the tasks. The human relationship continues to be valid and reasonable inasmuch as there is an exchange of needs.

Respect

Respect your spouse and whatever they are as a person. You have to respect the effort they are making in the relationship and even the effort they are making in their professional lives. Also, you need to acknowledge their feelings and respect every bit of it. They are people with feelings that can be destroyed by the most important people in their life: you. You are also responsible in boosting their self-worth and self-esteem. Trusting their abilities will boost their confidence toward acting their best and in believing that someone respects and appreciate the effort they are making, someone very significant to their happiness. They would like to come home every day just to meet you, because they are sure to meet a pleasant person at home. Your spouse also needs to be pampered to feel special.

How can you make them happy?

In your little ways, how can you contribute in making your spouse feel better? What would you do to make their day look brighter than it is?

As a married person, you have to contemplate on these kind of questions every morning. If you cannot take the time to brainstorm and actually take the step to do something no matter how small to make your spouse's life easier, then you don't deserve to be happy in your marriage. Never be too busy to remain Significant to the happiness of your partner and you will have a long lasting relationship.

You Vs Your Spouse

It is not a competition

People think marriage is a competition about who should become the happiest, but real marriage is the ability to recognize that the other person needs to be as happy as you are. It is the practice of making sure the other person is also happy. You can't be happy alone and find fulfilment in that happiness. Share your happiness with your spouse. Also, stay away from pushing blames toward your partner. Always look at the bright side of their actions even as you hope for them to become better.

Kill the ego

Kill the ego before the ego ruin your relationship. People don't ruin relationships, ego ruins relationship. Spouses need to work in making sure they keep up with each other, remain humble when necessary, take blames, be able to apologize and also correct when there is a need for correction. Yes, you will argue, there is no doubt to that. But you have to be careful not to allow your ego to stay in-between the solution of the problem and your marriage.

Actually say something

Do not assume that your partner will just understand how you are feeling or what you don't want. Your partner cannot read your mind. You have to actually talk about your feelings in details before your feelings will be understood. If you are sad or unhappy, talk things out with your spouse instead of becoming resentful or unforgiving. Even when you argue, know that you can only argue about a specific problem—the problem that is bothering you. Do not walk away from your partner, and try as much as possible to eliminate malice.

Have what you love and love what you have

Before marriage everything about your choice of person or character is about "having **what you love.**" You were given "the chance to **choose** and **have** what you love. But marriage is the beginning of a new dawn for love. You have to learn to start loving **what you have.**" Be contented with what you have and work in helping what you have to improve to the best of your imaginations. Part of loving what you have is the ability to give proper attention so that this person will become a better person. You are also what they have, and you can't deny them what they supposed to have. This rule will keep your mind aligned within the marriage atmosphere and you will begin to find ways to create happiness no matter of the challenges.

Hone your sense of humor

Crack more jokes with your partner. Marriage does not bring about the end of your sense of humor. You should try as much as possible to be playful with your spouse even as you try even harder to make them smile. This will enhance your relationship, and even once in a while your spouse will remember the reason they chose to marry you. Let your marriage become an adventurous journey for as long as possible.

Do The Impossible

Do not limit the possibilities for learning from each other

There is no way you can figure out everything about this person at once or within the first 5 or 10 years of marriage. There are a lot you don't know about their behaviors, impulse and potentials that you need to make effort to get to know. This calls for consistent interest in them even when it seems like you have already talked about everything. Even if you have to fake tolerating their talkativeness, try harder to figure out something interesting, so that you could automatically boost your interest towards them.

Go after a challenge

Signup for the gym together, go for hiking, join a sports team. Sweating together as a couple doing outdoor activities and sports helps in improving intimacy. Brainstorm and come up with physical activities that might present some challenges, then make plans to participate with your spouse. Create the opportunity to be close mentally and physically with your partner. Doing such things twice a week will provide the affection you need, and you will learn better things about your partner than you have ever learned.

Love and like

"Love is closely tied to lust, and the desire for the opposite sex. Like, is all about accepting someone as a friend, where his or her personalities is pleasant to you and you would always like them around." You have to go beyond love to **liking** your partner. You have to start liking their ideologies, their way of solving problems and how they react to challenging situations. It is very important that couples go beyond attraction to be able to find partnership within themselves. This is one of the best secrets for achieving a long-lasting and satisfying marriage. Because love can fade, but likeness or friendship remains forever, regardless of their flights and fallouts.

Date each other

Turn every Friday night your date night. Go to the park together, plan for a picnic, bed and breakfast, or just a trip to a fancy restaurant. Also, you can choose cheaper ways to spend time together by walking in nature and finding a secluded place outside your home where you can talk about yourselves. Also, visiting a new restaurant in the city every month will keep the passion and you will never get tired of each other.

Final Words

Marriage is a battle field of happiness, but there is never a guarantee of constant happiness. You have to understand and be comfortable with the fact that you will be sad somethings; you will cry and even regret the whole idea of marriage. But one thing is certain, there will also be some brighter days, and you need to cherish them. Instead of whining and worrying about the bad days, understand the things that brought about the bad days and avoid these things. Then understand the things that brought about some of your best days and work tirelessly in cultivating them. Every day will be a new day for a new discovery and you will never get tired of the journey.

Other Books by the Same Author

1. <u>200 Ways to Seduce Your Husband:</u> How to Boost Your Marriage Libido and Actually Enjoy Sex: A Couple's Intimacy Guide

2. <u>232 Questions for Couples</u>: Romantic Relationship Conversation Starters for Connecting, Building Trust, and Emotional Intimacy

3. <u>Communication in Marriage:</u> How to Communicate Effectively With Your Spouse, Build Trust and Rekindle Love

4. <u>Anger Management in Marriage:</u> Ways to Control Your Emotions, Get Healed of Hurts & Respond to Offenses (Overcome Bad Temper)

5. <u>100 Ways to Cultivate Intimacy in Your Marriage</u>: How to Improve Communication, Build Trust and Rekindle Love

6. <u>40 Bible Verses to Pray Over Your Husband and Marriage:</u> Powerful Scriptural Prayers for Protection, Guidance, Wisdom, Companionship, Commitment, Healing, and Deliverance

7. <u>Sexual Intimacy in Marriage:</u> 100 Facts Nobody Ever Told You About Sex and Romance [FREE BOOK]

8. <u>How to Build Trust in a Relationship:</u> Powerful Ways to Rebuild Effective Communication, Resolve Conflict, Improve Intimacy, And Avoid Betrayal

9. <u>How to Deal with Husband's Pornography Addiction:</u> Powerful Ways To Help Your Spouse To Overcome & Recover Completely, While Improving Your Sexual Intimacy

10. <u>How to Deal with A Difficult Spouse:</u> Regain Control, Living with a Demanding, Manipulative, and Unappreciative Partner

11. How to Repair a Broken Marriage: Get Back On Your Feet, Bring Back the Lost Passion, And Cultivate a Better Relationship

Printed in Great Britain
by Amazon